THE WORLD'S
72 TOUGHEST GOLF HOLES

TOM HEPBURN
SELWYN JACOBSON

PRICE/STERN/SLOAN
Publishers, Inc., Los Angeles
1986

Acknowledgements

Concept: Tom Hepburn and Selwyn Jacobson
Text: Tom Hepburn
Artwork: Tom Folwell, John Cole, Grant Hannah
Illustrations: Rod Proud
Design: Judy Hungerford
Production: Selwyn Jacobson
Typeset in Fenice by Jacobson Graphic Communications Group
Printed in Hong Kong by Colorcraft Ltd

Published by
Price/Stern/Sloan Publishers, Inc.
410 North La Cienega Boulevard,
Los Angeles, California 90048.

Photographic materials supplied by:

Colour Library International (London)
Tony Stone Associates (London)
The Photo Library (Australia)
Douglass Baglin Photography (Australia)
Orion Press (Japan)
Photo Researchers Inc (U.S.A.)
Picturepoint Ltd (London)
A.P.A. Ltd (Singapore)
R. Ian Lloyd Ltd (Singapore)
Banyan Products Ltd (Singapore)

Robin Smith Ltd (New Zealand)
Barnaby's Ltd (London)
Color Library Ltd (South Africa)
Gerald Cubitt — Photography (South Africa)
Ministry of Foreign Affairs (South Africa)
Masterfile (Canada)
Color Library International (Canada)
International Press (New Zealand)
Photobank Ltd (New Zealand)

Third Printing — August 1986

ISBN 0-8431-1062-7

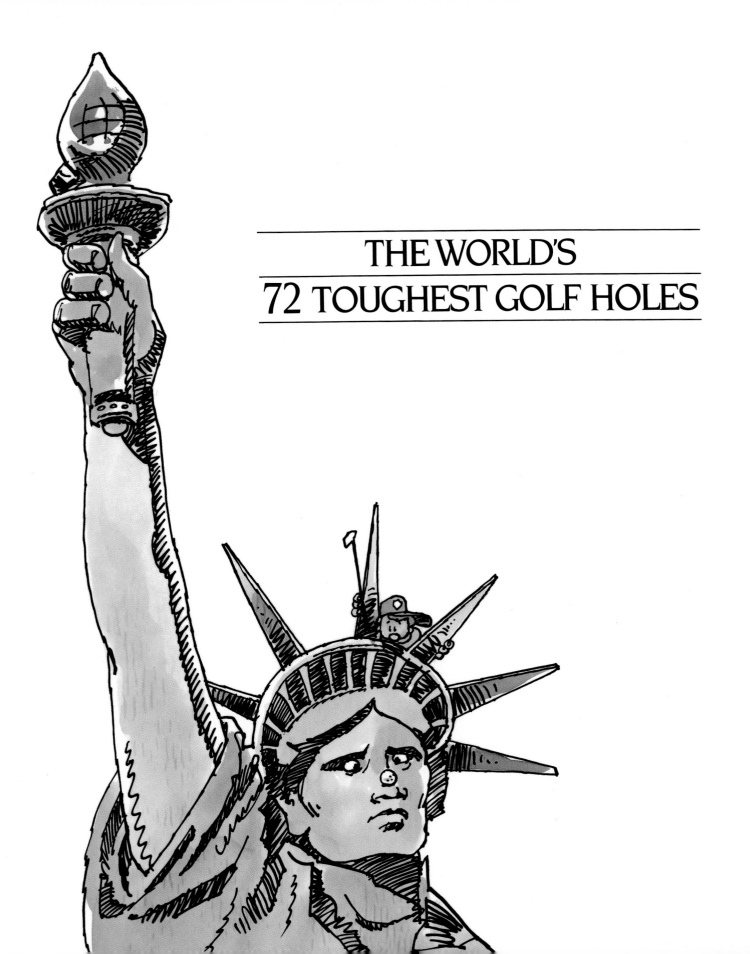

THE WORLD'S
72 TOUGHEST GOLF HOLES

Desert — Queensland, Australia

CONTENTS

Huka Falls — New Zealand

INTRODUCTION

Every golfer's dream — to meander leisurely around the world, playing the famous courses, swapping yarns in the 19th's, money no object, no wife insisting you get back by six to mow the lawn . . .

But even a golfer's Heaven has its corresponding Hell. This book helps to redress the rather unfair balance created by the hundreds — nay, thousands — of golfing publications which deliberately fail to highlight the *real* hazards of the game.

Be warned though; once you begin your odyssey to the 72 Holes of Hell inside, you'll never unwrap a new ball again without a qualm, or pull a club out of your bag without a third, even fourth thought.

Our book, inevitably, concentrates on those areas where golf courses are most prolific. But it would be grossly unfair if we did not attempt to highlight some of the further-flung clubs of the world. (For the all-comers club flinging record, read Samson McBaffie's *Trap Tantrums & Fairway Furies — a Personal Explanation*, from Lee Trevino University Press, $29.95).

After much deliberation concerning sequence of holes — should they be geographical, arranged as true 18's, in order of height above sea level, or . . ? We have presented them in four groups, each of which represents the total variety any first class course should offer.

We trust you will enjoy a gentle stroll through our pictorial golfing paradise. One thing we *are* certain of — when next you step up to your own local 1st tee, it will be with light heart. It *has* to be easy in comparison!

Golf Holes   1 — 18

THE VALHALLA GOLF CLUB'S
6th

---

880 yards
par 4

HEADS I WIN

BACK IN THE GOOD OLD DAYS, when Valhalla still had rooms to rent, golf was the only real man's game available. Your average Viking, after a hard campaign of conquest, pillage and rape, needed some outlet for his high spirits. Not surprisingly, he turned to golf, and most famous among such men is surely the legendary Snede Samsson. You'll remember at once the Pro's Edda describing how he'd take the Fat Cats of the Fjords? Pro for many years at this very club, Snede as a youngster would challenge any Viking to a sudden death playoff at this hole, the mark to use a full set of clubs and Samsson to play with but a putter and his favorite two-handed twin-bladed driving axe. After getting a good laugh at his opponent's inevitably short drive, Snede would swing his driver, lop off the head of the unfortunate Viking and without grounding his club belt the head clear across the water and onto the green — often to putt out in 3. Yes, one of the great golfers of all time!

Geiranger Fjord — Norway

THE WHAKAREWAREWA COUNTRY CLUB'S 18th

375 yards
par 4

PUDDLES

VISITORS TO WHAKAREWAREWA'S demanding course are (almost) always briefed before teeing off by a club official with the cautionary tale of Bessie Peasemarch and are careful to avoid getting into the local hazard which has become internationally synonymous with trouble — hot water! Less than accurate drives tend to finish nestling in one of the myriad pools of scalding foam emanating from the famous Pohutu Geyser, a feature of this hole. If the golfer is not extremely fast off his mark with a fairway iron he may well approach his second only to find the ball partially dissolved in the horrendously hot water (out of which incidentally he must play the lie if less than 30in deep — *Local rule 31d*).

The Club's membership, never large and dwindling alarmingly until Senior Geyserkeeper McGregor Horomia moved the green farther forward, away from the actual blowhole, has now steadied and visitors are once again welcome to sample the full 18 holes in comparative safety.

Rotorua — New Zealand

THE AYRES ROCK GOLF CLUB'S

6th

240 yards
par 4

BALL-BREAKER

THE BIGGEST ROCK in the world *has* to have something special about its golf course, and Ayres Rock doesn't let the visitor down. The trilogy of holes up here near the top of this vast boulder, the 6th, 7th and 8th, are known locally as "The Ballbreakers" — and not just because even a 100 compression Top-Flite can only take a couple of bounces before showing signs of a smile!

There are only so many alternatives for the golfer unwilling to go for the green in one, and many the foursome who, golf bags dragging dejectedly behind them, can be seen heading back to the Clubhouse, not a playable ball left between them!

CROC TRAP

Ayres Rock — Northern Territories, Australia

THE CHITTENANGO FALLS GOLF CLUB'S

8th

---

380 yards
par 4

THE POOLS

LET NONE DOUBT THE EFFICACY of water as a natural hazard — and when it is in great abundance, such as here at Chittenango Falls, no need to add blue dye for the TV cameras, nor indeed to paint the grass green — even in summer.

An intriguing local rule here concerns the three tees. Not (as you may think) Championship, Men's and Ladies', these markers are graded to allow for recent rainfall, ensuing depth of water and speed of torrent. For example, a long dry spell means more carry to the green, thus the White Tees are used; but woe betide a topped drive from even the Yellows during a Spring thaw!

Chittenango Falls — New York, America

THE AYUTTHAYA COUNTRY CLUB'S
12th

370 yards
par 4

TEMPLE TEMPER

PROBABLY THE OLDEST GOLF CLUB in Southeast Asia, the venerable greens of Ayutthaya have many a torrid tale to tell — if one can but read them properly!

Our photograph shows the ruins of the old Clubhouse, destroyed not once but twice ('59 and '67) by a band of irritated Burmese, refused playing privileges because of their unsatisfactory standard of dress. However, despite the razing of the buildings, the course itself remains immaculate as ever, offering as fine a test of good golf as any in Thailand. And to this day, though visitors from over the Burmese border are allowed (all else being equal) to play, they are *not* permitted inside the Clubhouse!

Ayutthaya — Thailand

THE COLERAINE & DISTRICT GOLF CLUB'S 5th

605 yards
par 5

GIANT'S FAIRWAY

THIS DECEPTIVELY TRICKY hole has been the undoing of many a promising round, yet seldom could any golfers have been so cheerfully tolerant of their bad luck as Ephraim and Thaddeus Paisley, who came simultaneously and spectacularly to grief here during the first round of the Ballycastle and Milligan Point Licensed Barkeepers' Annual Fifty Best Customers Tournament.

Sensibly fortifying themselves en route from judiciously placed kegs of draft Guinness (with best wishes from the sponsors), the Paisley twins (no relation) arrived mellow if unsteady at the 5th tee. Ephraim, who'd never been properly reconnected to his left foot (a legacy from The Troubles) failed to cope with the awkwardly contoured fairway and soon found himself firmly wedged in a cleft. Always the gentleman, Thaddeus hastened to his aid but in trying to pry Ephraim free with his putter, he too became inextricably stuck. Working on the theory that if they could just relax enough they'd slide free, the lads proceeded to relax as much as they could. In an impromptu (if slurred) after dinner speech that evening, Thaddeus thanked the sponsors, whose continued supply of lubricating fluids had contributed so successfully to their final release.

Giants Causeway — Ireland

THE SERRE-PONÇON COUNTRY CLUB'S 4th

250 yards
par 3

GENDARME

PLAYING WITH POLICEMEN is one of the slightly unnatural hazards encountered by golfers everywhere, but in provincial France such an event takes on an extra *frisson* as "la peur du gendarme" often lasts well into adult life. This fascinating hole, not unexpectedly known locally as "the gendarme" (from its uncanny resemblance to a uniformed dummy directing traffic) was for this reason the scene of considerable embarrassment to a visiting foursome of British clergymen. Losing their way, as men of this vocation so often do, on the long third, the group finally stumbled on a small village where they sensibly inquired at the local police station where they might find the fourth hole. Alas, their French was imperfect and the request "Où est le trou du gendarme?"** resulted in their being thrown in jail. They were released only when they gave their names as Hogan, Snead, Ballasteros and Palmer — a little white lie which any God would forgive.

** translation on request

Serre-Ponçon — France

THE NUMINBAH VALLEY COUNTRY CLUB'S

14th

---

205 yards
par 3

CEC'S POOL

WHEN CECIL HARDBOTTLE emigrated from his rented, rat-infested hovel on the banks of the Manchester Ship Canal to Springbrook, Queensland , he was only 79. Yet within a few years his name was legion at the N.V.G.C. The slowest player in the Club, he was too deaf to hear cries of "fore!" and too difficult to let anyone play through. His was the voice raised loudest in argument in the 19th; and his hand only went into his pocket when he wanted to blow his nose. But one day, having slipped across the nearby border to sinful New South Wales for a dirty weekend at the Knobby's Creek Club Med, Cec cut loose and invested in a Lotto ticket.

It was first prize, and in a flood of alcoholic benevolence Hardbottle returned to Springbrook where he had designed and installed the unique walkway and raft tee seen in our picture, making possible a previously hard to par hole. The special pulley allows the raft to be drawn up to the green and par can be changed to either 4 or 5, depending on the day. Cec, overcome by his own generosity, decided it must have been the heat and returned home to Salford, rich enough to buy his own hovel.

Numinbah Valley — Queensland, Australia

THE BLACK TUSK MTN. GOLF & CLIMBING CLUB'S 8th

---

390 yards
par 4

TSK! TSK!

THE TROUBLE WITH USING elephants instead of Snowcats (apart from trying to turn a mahout into a decent caddy) is having to get off and on so many times during a round. The big advantage, of course, is their ability to find balls otherwise irretrievably plugged into deep snow. Hannibal McBaffie, on his world-wide demonstration tour introducing the then contentious Snow Wedge*, offered a brilliant solution to this problem when playing here at Black Tusk. His (patent pending) telescopic shaft, extending at the touch of a button up to 13 ft, allows most on-the-fairway shots to be played from the howdah. How dahs he do it? You may well ask. The answer is, not always!

An early attempt at an approach shot on this very hole resulted in his mechanism misfiring and the clubhead being propelled at great velocity down into deep snow. Alas, a minor avalanche followed, rendering McBaffie clubless, his elephant legless and the 8th hole teeless.

"Play Winning Shots from Drifts" by James Braid McBaffie should be published soon.

Black Tusk Mt. — British Columbia, Canada

THE HERON ISLAND GOLF CLUB'S
18th

---

230 yards
par 3

RAY'S A LAUGH

THIS VERY OLD PHOTOGRAPH (the clubhouse bar has since been considerably extended and the toilets re-roofed) shows just one of the variegated holes offered by this fine Barrier Reef links.

As befits the largest coral reef in the world, the hazards here are often in proportion — for example, the gigantic manta ray which brought an end to the superlative series of 8 consecutive birdies by "Toc" (Tropic of Capricorn) Teague, the club's snorkeling champion since 1883.

As was his wont, Toc was skimming the surface towards the 18th green after another first class tee shot when he espied, nestling on the seabed 30 fathoms below, what appeared to be a near-new B-52. Diving to check it out for smiles and frowns, Toc collided with the enormous ray whose tail tickled him so unmentionably that he let go his clubs and had to surface for a change of underwear. Six minutes later, still laughing, he conceded the hole. A titillating tale!

Heron Island — Queensland, Australia

THE ARCHES GOLF CLUB'S
4th

360 yards
par 4

FALLEN ARCHES

WITH THE BEST WILL in the world our researchers could not ignore this marvelous golf hole from the redoubtable group of tight little courses scattered over the Arches National Monument's 34,249.94 acres (it was originally thought that there were 34,250, but allowance had to be made for an Indian Reservation). In fact it was Chief Researcher Bledisloe McTuft who was responsible for the naming of the hole during the very first round shot at this short but tricky par 4. His congenital foot ailment struck savagely and suddenly, causing him to drop a good two inches on the left side halfway through his downswing, top the ball under the Arch and spoil an otherwise excellent card. His bellow of combined outrage and agony was construed by his deafish partner to be "FALLEN ARCH!" but a passing threesome were to agree later at the 19th that "fallen", though fairly close, was not *quite* the word used . . .

Arches National Monument — Utah, America

THE CAPE POINT GOLF CLUB'S 13th

320 yards
par 4

SEA HERE

POSSIBLY THE WORLD'S MOST EXACTING "target" green, Cape Point's 13th offers a last local challenge before the final five easy-ish holes back round to the Cape of Good Hope and the clubhouse.

But a word of warning! In going for the green with the drive, take great care to assess carefully the prevailing wind — a local factor which demands proper club choice. Indeed, a special rule here allows caddies to hold onto players during the tee shot where the wind exceeds 75 mph — far too many matches have had to be abandoned because of careless golfers allowing themselves to be blown off the ledge!

Yet in making life tough for the low handicappers, the 13th also offers the duffer something to remember: depending on the extent of hook or slice, a ball may be lost forever in either of two seas. Ask yourself, how many golfers can truthfully say they played their drive into the Atlantic, their next into the Indian Ocean?

Cape Point — South Africa

THE BALI GOLF AND COUNTRY CLUB'S 12th

285 yards
par 4

PADDY'S WAGON

IRISH GOLFERS in Bali are thicker on the ground than many may think (which is more than one can say about the fairway rough, but that's a water buffalo of a different color, as they say in Indonesia!). In fact it was indeed such an animal which was responsible for elderly Shamus O'Chakkri's failure to win (for the third time and thus outright) the Senior Champs back in '27. O'Chakkri, two under the card here at the 12th, had played a fine approach to within birdie distance of the pin when suddenly a farmer appeared with his water buffalo dragging a cart filled with dung and sewage and proceeded to plow up the green! Understandably miffed, Shamus emigrated to Waikabubak and opened a second hand batik supplies store. Yes, even the great and joyous game of golf has its sadder moments.

Rice Paddies — Bali

SNOWDONIA COUNTRY CLUB'S
3rd

580 yards
par 5

MINER KEY

WHEN THE MASSED (Welsh-speaking) choirs of the Llanwrst and Llangynog Collieries held their annual golf tournament up on Snowdonia's icy acres last year, such was their sense of relief at being high in the fresh air instead of down in the pits that they spontaneously burst into a rendition of the famous *Caddie's Chorus* from Baffierdi's *"St. Andrew's Passion"*.

Alas they failed to allow for potential echoes, and their brief moment of glory was later assessed as having caused two avalanches, three heart attacks and fourteen duffed shots. The third tee, focal point of this debacle, now carries a warning sign forbidding the call of "fore", as the inevitable multiplication often confuses.

Snowdonia — Wales

THE NAHANNI COUNTRY CLUB'S 15th

305 yards
par 4

YOUR SLIP IS . . .

THE SENSIBLE GOLFER will play safe here and place his drive onto the Ladies Tee where, though he must play the lie, the approach is ideal for making par. The attractive Virginia Falls offers a pleasing backdrop to this cunningly contrived golf hole — drop being, in the case of willing though unsullied Priscilla Pointdexter, the *mot juste.*

Prissie, on her way to tee off, had slipped on a wet plank and in a moment was hanging from the swing bridge by one hand, the other clutching her new bag of clubs. Her partner, handsome Lester LeStrange, sensibly yelled "Drop 'em!" but in her understandable panic Prissie misunderstood his intentions . . .

No, this *isn't* why they're known as "Virginia Falls" — but nearly!

Virginia Falls — Nahanni National Park, N.W.T. Canada

THE GOREME GOLF CLUB'S 16th

420 yards
par 4

'ATTATURK!

UP AND AROUND THE half mile level on the arid Anatolian Plateau nestles this little Turkish Delight of a golf course. Though generally conservative in layout it gains entry into our World's 72 by dint of an event which took place here on the scintillating 16th.

In October '22 during the Lake Van to Lake Tuz one-club one-ball cross-country tournament, two local high handicappers, Trevinian and Arnieian, were hesitating on the 16th tee when they were passed by a golfer moving at ten times their pace. "My God, who's that?" gasped Trev. "If he keeps moving at that speed he'll soon be leading the field."

"Mustapha Kemal," grunted Arnie in reply.

"Wish *I'd* thought to hire one!" muttered Trev.

[Note: In addition to its place in golf history, this dialogue has been nominated for inclusion in *The World's Worst Puns*, to be published later this year.]

Goreme Tal — Turkey

THE TONGAPORUTU MUNICIPAL LINK'S
8th

390 yards
par 4

"TROIS SOEURS" TROUSERS

ANTOINETTE, BRIGITTE AND CHOUX-CHOUX, the famous golfing daughters of old Tamati 'Tutaenui' Teremoana, were collectively responsible for the curious name of this hole during a particularly windy day some years ago. When their French mother Rangi (née d'Urville) emigrated from Akaroa to Taranaki she was quickly wooed and won by fast talking Tamati, and after presenting him the following summer with triplets, she devoted the rest of her life to teaching them all she knew about short irons. Known far and wide during their competitive years as the "Trois Soeurs", the "Three Sisters" of Tongaporutu played as they lived and loved — together! On the windy day in question they'd made up a foursome with Percival Muffin, the Club's gigolo, and here on the blustery 8th the girls, feeling like a frolic, decided to depants him. Alas, the wind proved too strong and no sooner were the garments held triumphantly aloft than they blew gaily out to sea, leaving Percival no option but to shuffle awkwardly back to the Clubhouse, scorecard judiciously placed. His plea to the Greens Committee that it was all the fault of the triplets met with derision and thanks to his poor French pronounciation the scene of his discomfiture was thenceforth known as "Trois Soeurs Trousers".

Tongaporutu — New Zealand

THE BORROWDALE COUNTRY CLUB'S 13TH

380 yards
par 4

ROGUE HERRING

WHEN OLD WALPOLE HERRING, who drank 12 pints of cider a night down at the Drunken Duck, took his near-new set of matching McBaffies to Keswick market and accepted the first price offered, there was many a sharp intake of breath heard in the town.

Everyone at the Club knew Wally, yet no one had ever played a round with the old loner! He'd be seen out on the course in all weathers, snow or rain, mist or sun, morning and evening, thrashing away according to first this book of instruction, then that one, until the never to be forgotten day when he broke 100!

Totally unhinged by this — his previous best had been 186 (with 14 "gimmes"), Wally sold his clubs and vowed never to swing at a ball again. Yet he still strides the 13th, eyes wild and staring, hair long and lank, clothes filthy and ragged, mumbling a semi-coherent question at anyone he meets, "My clubs, my dear dear irons, my lovely sweet woods, have you seen them?"

Borrowdale — England

THE RUSHMORE GOLF AND COUNTRY CLUB'S
8th

290 yards
par 3

HEAD HEIGHTS

NEVER AN EASY HOLE to par, this exciting challenge on Rushmore's lesser known "East 18" first came into prominence back in '27 when four keen amateurs George, Tom, Abe and Ted (at that time mere weekday members) each holed out in one during the same round *and with the same mashie-niblick!* So impressed was the Match Committee with this sterling achievement that they commissioned busts of the famous foursome for the President's Bar mantelshelf in the 19th. Unfortunately, Arbuthnot Mulliner, the club's sculptor, though playing off a six, was also a bit deaf and misunderstood his instructions. Thus instead of four golfers immortalised in the President's Bar, four Presidents began to appear on the 8th hole — since 1941 a star attraction on the U.S.A. circuit.

Mt. Rushmore — South Dakota, America

THE MARAKOPA GOLF CLUB'S 14th

170 yards
par 3

SCOTCH MISSED

SAFE IN A CREVICE, cunningly tucked behind the cascades of water which make this a real hit or mist hole, rests a bottle of Scotia's finest fluid, its exact resting place known only to one man. Old Glen Dronagh, whose only contact with single figure golf for the past 30 years has been between the 1st and 4th holes (before he starts on his second bottle and his eyes are still functioning as a pair) likes to keep the odd medicinal drop secreted around his favorite course for he, like all of us, knows well that dread moment when, after perhaps bending the elbow too much the evening before, the head is lowered for the first putt. Time seems strangled; the ball jerks perceptibly sideways then, after growing smaller, fades at the edges; a fire engine and a train can be clearly heard colliding just behind the eyes; all is not well. But thanks to this and other liquid caches, old Dronagh has not failed to complete a carefree round since that awful day ten years ago when a sliced drive smashed the bottle here at the falls and he failed to putt out, claiming he was stymied by a herd of pink elephants.

Marakopa Valley — New Zealand

THE CAPE ST. FRANCIS COUNTRY CLUB'S
5th

410 yards
par 3

KATE'S LAST KISS

FROM WITLESS BAY round to Old Perlican the name Katarina Kelligrews struck fear into the heart of every golfer. Weighing in at around 300 lb. and standing 6' 2" in her golfing socks, "Kiss Me Kate", as she was known from her desperate attempts to attract a husband who could not only support, but outdrive her, seized every opportunity to show her appreciation of good play. Terrified big hitters would stay home rather than risk winning a cup and being kissed accordingly by Kate, who made a point of entering every major tournament open — and as she played off scratch, she qualified for most. But came the day, at last year's St. Francis Mixed Foursomes . . .

Playing the longish par 3 fifth, Kate saw her partner, bespectacled paper magnate Botwood J. Batt, nonchalantly drive the green with his 4-wood. Simple decorum forbids a detailed description of ensuing events but Botwood won the Longest Drive competition, offered his arm to Kate, and thereby trebled the men's membership of every Club within a day's drive. It's an ill wind.

Cape St. Francis — Newfoundland, Canada

SINGAPORE CENTRAL G.C's

1st - 6th

distance total 1165 yards all par 3's

BRIDGES OVER TROUBLED WATERS

IN THIS EXCITING CITY of hard workers, industrious executives and gifted entrepreneurs, where new buildings go up one every 10 minutes (or so taxi drivers think) and where 2½ million people live happily with each other on 210 sq miles — someone had to come up with Every Businessman's Answer to Stress . . .

From midday until 2 p.m. (more or less) those lucky first 50 tycoons who each forked over $265,500 to join this, the smallest yet most exclusive Golf Club in Southeast Asia, can relax, keep their short game in order and do business at the same time. Thanks to Sony's portable multi-channel, silicon-chipped radio-TV tee-holders (offered free with every membership, including 6 assorted-height tees) they can keep in touch with the international marketplace.

Life memberships (non-transferable) may be applied for, pending the death of an existing member. Apply in confidence to Mr T. K. Sang, Club Secretary, c/o Metro Shoe-Shine Dept., 106 Boon Keng Road.

City Centre – Singapore

THE CHAMONIX CLUB'S 14th

650 yards
par 6

BLANC CZECH

THE DECEPTIVELY LARGE GREEN here (1.3 acres) tends to make even experienced players underclub on the approach, though once on the green it's just a question of settling down to some steady work with the putter. Other holes offer other hazards, however, and many is the prominent visitor who has left his mark around the course.

Perhaps none was so infamous as that fine golf player from Czechoslovakia, Nikolaus Wenceslaus. Nicki was the only one from that terrible Christmas tournament in '07 not to make it back to the Clubhouse. Last seen heading resolutely into a snowstorm up the four mile ice field which forms the long 12th, dressed in his usual flamboyant all-white gear, he was never seen again. Today a pair of crossed baffies mark the spot where he was thought to have played his last fairway iron.

Mer de Glace — France

THE YELLOWSTONE GOLF CLUB'S

13th

650 yards
par 5

HOT PUTTS

THIS INTERESTING PHOTOGRAPH (snapped by bison addict Mrs. Sophie Q. Noakes) illustrates one of the perils of golfing in Nevada. An unsuspecting high handicapper (you can tell by his grip) has failed to take advantage of the free seismograph kits offered with every buggy hired at the Yellowstone clubhouse, and has been caught trying to putt out during a "blow".

Apart from ruining a set of clubs, and suffering third degree burns at the very least, the foolish fellow has probably spoiled an otherwise perfectly good round.

Yellowstone National Park — Wyoming, America

THE THINGVELLIR COUNTRY CLUB'S
5th

205 yards
par 3

THING ICE

SCOTTISH SLAVES almost certainly brought golf to Iceland around the second half of the ninth Century, but it was not really until that unforgettable occasion when Snorri Sturluson and Arni Palmersson grabbed the Pairs Final here at Thingvellir in 1258 that the game took a permanent grip on the populace.

Golf became the very stuff of which sagas were written, and Snorri's rhyming 3008 verse account of his last nine holes with Arni still ranks as one of the least known poems anywhere in the world.

Today, running along the banks of pretty Lake Thingvallavatn, is hole after breathtaking hole where each year (since the epic match) the Annual Broken Icicle Award is held, when the lads from the Hvannadalshnukur Links do battle with the locals, entertaining golfing aficionados from Vik to Raufarhofn.

Thingvellir — Iceland

THE KIMBERLEY COUNTRY CLUB'S
1st

180 yards
par 3

STONE ME!

"A HELL OF A WAY TO BEGIN A ROUND OF GOLF" — these propitious words uttered by Duggie Cronin when he played his grudge match against "Mad Mitch" McGregor in '99, are now engraved above the 19th's Members Bar in honor of the course record (still standing) he set that day of 102.

Cronin and McGregor so entertained the big gallery that a memorabilia museum was opened. Today a fine selection of Bushman art and Cape fauna take second place to a detailed, blow-by-blow account of how both men played — and halved — this arduous first hole in 37.

First-time visitors here are still offered the traditional free diamond if they get out in par. Astonishingly, no one has yet claimed the prize!

Kimberley, (Big Hole) — South Africa

THE FIORDLAND GOLF CLUB INC'S

8th

227 yards
par 3

DEVIL'S DROP

KEY TO PAR SCORING here is a very straight 5 wood/4 iron to the front of the green with plenty of stop on the ball. A too-low drive could result in running off the rear of the normally hard-surfaced green and the inevitable chip back up could lose a valuable stroke or two. Many top golfers claim this to be the most spectacular hole in the world, eclipsing the 18th at Pebble Beach for sheer beauty — not to mention need for pin-point accuracy. It was this need to hit straight which caused the downfall of little Lachlan Couth, the club's shortest player; he'd hit a fat 6 rather than an easier 5-iron, overswung, lost his balance off the tee and fallen to a ledge below. Thanks to his lack of stature he had to be pulled up by his niblick and was never the same again.

Milford Sound — New Zealand

THE MALAGA COUNTRY CLUB'S 12th

395 yards
par 3

BALLERO

THIS ATTRACTIVE if fairly straightforward little course never lacks for excitement, and for a very interesting reason — the back nine are laid out within a major bull-fighting arena. Each Sunday golf takes on a new meaning for those brave enough to play a full round, and when you hear the comment in the 19th "Did you see that amazing charge from the 15th!" you can be sure birdies had nothing to do with it. An intriguing local rule here states that "any golfer striking a bull, with club or ball, shall lose the hole and his ears".

Fortunately this is offset a little by players being allowed to carry a muleta as a 15th club. And visitors, if they've any sense, will take advantage of the caddierilleros who can advise not only on club choice, but where to stick them!

Torcal — Malaga, Spain

THE EIGER GOLF & ALPINE CLUB'S 7th

660 yards
par 5

DOG LEG

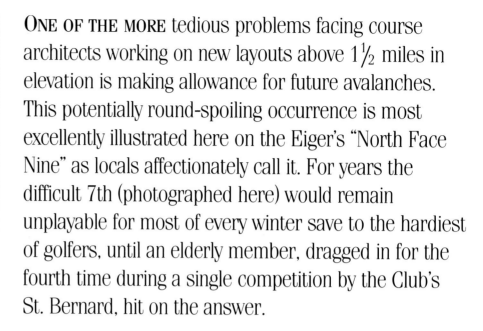

ONE OF THE MORE tedious problems facing course architects working on new layouts above 1½ miles in elevation is making allowance for future avalanches. This potentially round-spoiling occurrence is most excellently illustrated here on the Eiger's "North Face Nine" as locals affectionately call it. For years the difficult 7th (photographed here) would remain unplayable for most of every winter save to the hardiest of golfers, until an elderly member, dragged in for the fourth time during a single competition by the Club's St. Bernard, hit on the answer.

Simplicity itself! Fit a tiny radio transmitter to every ball and a receiver to the St. Bernard, and no matter how far a ball was carried off course, the faithful hound would seek it out and return it to where it was struck. Penalty stroke, of course, but at least players could complete their rounds.

Eiger – Switzerland

THE DURACK RANGES COUNTRY CLUB'S

9th (green) & 10th

420 yards
par 4 or 420 yards +
4 cans par 5

TOO HEY OR NOT TOO HEY

THIS IS THE QUESTION which brought the entire committee to blows, that fateful December in '36. The Clubhouse had never rung to such a cacophony of curses. Two ladies felt obliged to resign, and elderly Perseus McPugh had to be helped from his wheelchair.

The argument was, which beer to put on tap at the half-way house? Well, our photograph shows the answer, and its popularity may be judged by the fact that more 9-hole games of golf are played here than at any other Australian course. As the old dirge has it:

"There's nothing so fatal to good golf I fear,
Than to stop at the half-way and top up with beer."

Durack Ranges — Western Australia, Australia

THE NIAGARA GOLF AND BARRELLING CLUB'S
10th

440 yards
par 4

HORSESHOE SHUFFLE

MANY IS THE INTREPID low-handicapper (Blondini McBaffie, at his best down to a 3, springs to mind) who has dared attempt a Niagara tightrope crossing — on a bicycle, blindfolded, two-up, the list goes on. But never in the history of this famous hydroelectric plant has there been the likes of Adam "Ride 'em Cowboy" Beck (the first man to sell Niagara water to the Americans) whose avowed intent to play this risky hole while mounted on a horse started tongues wagging in the Members' Bar. The news spread fast; it was clear an immense crowd would attend and the secretary (himself a music lover) arranged for the Elk's Club barber shop quartet to sing a victory medley when Adam reached the green.

Unfortunately tee-off was delayed pending the departure of two high handicappers setting out in barrels and the quartet, their thirst exacerbated by the Falls, got into a case or two of Labatts fine product. When young Beck finally started (with an excellent 4-iron) they became confused and struck up an erratic version of "Harvest Moon". The nag supporting Adam, of Louisiana stock, understandably began a soft-shoe shuffle on the rope, lost his balance and . . . the rest is history.

Niagara Falls — Canada

THE LOCH EARN GOLF CLUB'S
16th

---

550 yards
par 5

HAIR CURLER

REMINISCENT OF THE LAST ICE AGE, winter sits heavily on the Scottish hills above Loch Earn. Yet at the first slant of sunshine through the Stygian gloom of the skies, out come the greensweepers, brooms flashing left and right. In no time greens and tees are cleared and golfers are out and about for another good day's sport.

Many players here carry curling stones with them. Sliding them up and down icy mountainsides is an excellent arm and finger exercise, conducive to an improved grip.

Care must be taken not to allow a stone to slide onto the putting surface. The 38 lb stone tends to make an unfortunate indentation which, this being Scotland, automatically becomes "rub of the green".

Loch Earn – Scotland

THE FLOWER POT ISLAND GOLF CLUB'S

15th

---

190 yards
par 3

GREEN GRASS

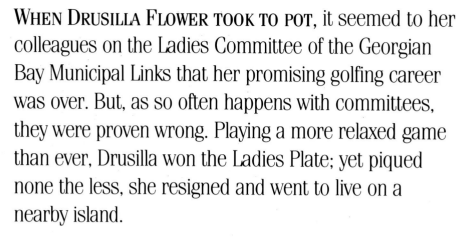

WHEN DRUSILLA FLOWER TOOK TO POT, it seemed to her colleagues on the Ladies Committee of the Georgian Bay Municipal Links that her promising golfing career was over. But, as so often happens with committees, they were proven wrong. Playing a more relaxed game than ever, Drusilla won the Ladies Plate; yet piqued none the less, she resigned and went to live on a nearby island.

The hermit's life did not appeal, however, and the old instincts rose again. Before long Drusilla had introduced her friends-in-exile to golf and formed the nucleus of a club. Inevitably a second 9 followed the first, to become the pleasant holiday resort so popular today. Named of course after its founding member — and the *raison d'etre* for her efforts! And this is still the only course known to have its greens planted with Drusilla's own unique blend.

Flower Pot Island — Ontario, Canada

THE MORENO GLACIER GOLF CLUB'S

18th

520 yards
par 5

TEHEULCHES

IN ONE OF HIS bi-weekly "Golf Gossip" columns, a popular feature of the *Gazeta de Buenos Aires* since June 7, 1810, Julio A. Roca, the preeminent Patagonian Amateur, wrote in glowing terms of the new clubhouse, designed by Mariana Moreno, himself, on the course's highest point.

Very much in the Costa Lotta style, then in vogue in Southern Spain, this fine edifice was a significant landmark until the terrible accident in '49 (read J. Thorpe's "A Bone-Idle Golfer in Patagonia" for the full, distressing story) and formed the perfect backdrop to the easy last hole here.

The only real drawback was that no one had designed a way of getting from the 18th green to the Clubhouse — at certain times of the year a bit of an inconvenience.

Moreno Glacier — Patagonia, Argentina

THE PHANGAN ISLAND GOLF CLUB'S
9th

406 yards
par 4

DROP SHOT

OF THE SIX championship courses which run down the Isthmus of Kra from Pran Buri in the north to Surat Tham in the south, none match the elegant architecture and design of this splendid complex at Phangan Island. Wafted by gentle breezes off the Gulf of Siam, the relaxed holiday atmosphere is exemplified by the Caddy Canoes which ferry golfers from green to green, the outstanding clubhouse facilities and, not least, some deceptively tricky holes like the ninth, seen in our photograph.

Here the ball must be struck well over the building below: onto the practice green is a penalty of 1, onto the Clubhouse roof is 2 strokes away and onto the head of a Club official is automatic loss of hole. Other than that, it's fun all the way.

Phangan Island – Malaysia

THE COLORADO COUNTRY CLUB'S
3rd

1045 yards
par 5

INDEPENDENCE MONUMENT

CHASTITY BELLTE-LOCKE was invited through a clerical error to play in the Invitational Pro-Am here in '27. (Mr B. Locke never did find out why he was neglected.) Nevertheless she gained more column inches in the local press than any golfer before her. A liberated lady, Chastity turned up for the event *without stays*! Her thus unhampered swing (no, she didn't wear one of those either) so inflamed her partner that he finally lost all control here on the third green, dropped to one knee and proposed. Unfortunately he knelt on Chastity's ball (well positioned for a birdie) pressing it into the ground and losing her the hole. Enraged, she (a) turned him down with a contemptuous snort, (b) felled him with a single fearsome blow from her putter and (c) so caused the hole from that day on to be known as Independence Monument.

Independence Monument — Colorado, America

THE CHOMO-LUNGMA COUNTRY CLUB'S 10th

490 yards
par 4

TENSING'S TEST

SNUG IN THE HIMALAYAN foothills, high on the Nepal-Tibet border, lies perhaps the most spectacular golf course in the world. Perspective here is the big problem — viz. the 10th in our picture, where the tee shot must be played over the clubhouse. As much carry as possible is recommended!

The popular Tibetan circuit pro, Lobsang "Ed" Tensing (nearly made the cut in the 1947 Lhasa Open), gave his name to this hole in 1953. As guest captain of the Ladies Team in their annual Stableford derby with neighboring Kanchenjunga Golf Club his backswing on his second shot, a niblick to the green, caught a sleeping Yeti in the abominables, rendering the poor beast even less of a legend than it was before.

Mt. Everest — Nepal

THE WAT PHRA KAEO ROYAL AND ANCIENT GOLF CLUB'S

18th

502 yards
par 5

ELEPHANT'S GRAVEYARD

THIS FINE EXAMPLE of "modified" 19th century European architecture is surely one of the world's most impressive clubhouses! The W.P.K.R.A. (often mistaken by visiting Americans for a radio station) also boasts Bangkok's only locker room designed to cater to elephants. These intelligent "caddiphants" as they are known locally have been trained to trumpet "fore!", to tread softly around the greens, and can if required, crush offensive clubs which have caused a particularly bad round. Thus the intriguing name of the 18th, a graveyard of woods and irons. The lush grass on the greens here is the product of much diligent watering by the 2436 assistant greenkeepers — a credit to their profession.

Watt Phra Kaeo Temple — Thailand

THE SLIEVE LEAGUE CLIFF GOLF CLUB'S
14th

---

220 yards
par 3

YORKER

FEW IRISH GOLF COURSES (if any) owe their titles to the drunken exploits of a prominent — thus un-named — Yorkshire rugby team. Slieve has that dubious privilege.

It was late in '53 when the bus with 13 good men and true, a few drinking officials and a bevy of beauties collected in Ilkley, took a wrong turn and, many brown ales later, found itself by an attractive rocky coastline which did not at all resemble Pontefract, their intended destination. Here they were met by a group of hurlers and after the initial confusions had been cleared up and a few convivial drinks downed, they all repaired to the local municipal links for a round of golf.

Locals agree the course has never been the same since, and that it was only reasonable to rename it in honor of that incredible debacle. Some of the Yorkshire lads still wonder about the big river they crossed, on the way to Pontefract!

Slieve League Cliffs — Ireland

THE YOSEMITE COUNTRY CLUB'S 9th

410 yards
par 4

WATER PITY

JUDICIOUS USE OF NATURAL water is always a hallmark of competent course architecture, and here layout expert Jose Mitty, younger brother of Walt, whose final unsuccessful leap led to the naming of the falls, not to mention the building of the bridge, used the natural terrain to add a dash of piquancy to the hole. On certain days, spray — and therefore a potentially slippery club — must be contended with, but the well-watered green will almost always hold even a low ball. Jose, who was club captain during the famous flood of '03, suffered from a "sympathetic" bladder and seldom made the swing bridge before succumbing to the call of the falls. While attempting a spot of mild relief he was caught unawares by a flash flood and swept to his doom. The course, though named in his honor, carries the unusual spelling above. The Mitty brothers, though fine golf architects, were — alas — illiterate.

Yosemite National Park — California, America

THE PUNAKAIKI GOLF AND DIVING CLUB'S
16th

200 yards
par 3

THE "BLOW" HOLE

THE DUAL TALENTS required by regular players at this old-established club on the west coast of New Zealand are often called into use, as the more-precarious-than-some tees and green of this fine golf hole indicate. Erroneously believed by many to be an Indian form of Bath Bun, Punakaiki is in fact the maiden name of Blodwyn Herewini who, single-handed, built the bridge over to the Ladies Tee, thus saving herself and her colleagues many an arduous climb. Indeed Blodwyn it was who in the final of the President's Cup, while negotiating her way down to the tee from the dogleg 17th (seen just below the green), found herself collected by a powerful waterspout and deposited, golf cart and all, back by the 16th pin where she ruined a crucial birdie putt for her sister Thuvia. The two ladies have not spoken to each other since.

Punakaiki — New Zealand

THE KLUANE COUNTRY CLUB'S
4th

750 yards
par 5

LUNACY

LONG BEFORE Midnight Mixed Foursomes became the 'in' game at Kluane, local golfers, frustrated by a shortish season (usually June through October unless further curtailed by inclement weather) would take advantage of every daylight hour to squeeze in a game or two. Thanks to the 20-hour day, members often managed four rounds before being forced inside by failing light.

But however this laid-back style of golf may have suited the elderly or the amputees, the more dedicated player — like young Bledisloe 'Bled the Sled' Chukchi — preferred to make good and proper use of his golfing time. Restricted by the demands made by his position as Senior Signalman on the busy Whitehorse-Skagway Railroad, Bled managed to whip his dog team up to his Club only four or five days a week. Despairing of ever getting in more than his four rounds per day, Bled was excited when he learned a lunar eclipse was due.

Our photograph shows the foursome he gathered together playing the heady 4th and we are pleased to record that Bled, partnered by big Bob 'Kodiak' Campbell took 'London' Jack and Wee Bobbie Service — for a considerable sum!

Kluane National Park — Yukon, Canada

THE DOLOMITES COUNTRY CLUB'S 17th

470 yards
par 4

IL DOLOROSO

AS ONE MIGHT EXPECT in Europe, many of the golf courses are redolent with history. Some indeed are red for another reason — blood! Yes, sad to say, Italian clubs *have* been raised in anger, and on occasion with good reason. Consider the intriguing case of Bonaparte (famous artilleryman) vs. Finione (famous chef) and their grudge match here at D.C.C. Irritated beyond measure by Bonaparte's pompous pronouncements concerning elevation of green, striking force of clubhead, weight of ball, trajectory and wind speed, Finione buckled down and thrashed his employer.

Enraged and humiliated, Bonaparte called up his favorite cannon *La Bearnaise* and proceeded to annihilate the course (and unfortunate players) hole by hole. Today evidence of his pique may be still seen in the fairways here at the 17th. Even the clubhouse was destroyed, but members confidently expect it to be rebuilt soon. Work, as may be seen in our photograph, has already begun on the new pro shop.

Dolomites — Italy

THE MORIALTA GOLF CLUB'S
5th

360 yards
par 4

SHEER LUCK

SHERLOCK HOLMES, in his unpublished monograph entitled "Random Thoughts on the Myriad Possibilities of Ministering Mayhem on Golf Courses", was careful to avoid mentioning his handicap. Even Watson, that devout recorder of Holmes' most interesting cases, hadn't a clue, though for the good Doctor that was about par for the course! (Perhaps, had he accompanied the great detective to South Australia in his pursuit of the dreaded Moriarty, he would never have had to invent the apparent "death" at the Reichenbach Falls.)

It seems Moriarty, trapped at last near the tee at the short 5th here and already 6 over the card, was forced to lock putters with his old antagonist. Wrestling savagely, they toppled over the Falls — and only one man crawled ashore. But which one?

The reader must draw his own conclusions, assisted perhaps by the words of the only observer to the above scene — a one-eyed aboriginal caddy with a faulty understanding of English. A final clue — the name he mumbled till the day he died was adopted as the new name of the golf course!

Morialta Falls — South Australia

THE THULE COUNTRY CLUB'S 17th

680 yards
par 5

BEAR BALLS

FOR MANY YEARS the favorite course of local U.S. Defense personnel, Thule's remarkable group of tame polar bears can add a soupçon of spice to what might otherwise be an uneventful round of golf.

The bears, trained to retrieve balls which skid into the water or become embedded in ice (this often happens when the temperature drops below -60°F) seldom attack golfers. It is recommended however not to indulge in too many practice swings in their vicinity, as an erratic backswing has in the past (K. Rasmussen, 1910) been misconstrued by a pregnant female.

Arctic

THE GIZEH GOLF CLUB INC'S
4th

---

486 yards
par 4

CHEOP-CHEOP

SPHINXES IN VARIOUS shapes and forms were common throughout the ancient Near East and Greece, often represented as the destructive agent of the Gods. Here at Gizeh, some time ago when the course was recently formed and had but 9 holes, legend has it that the local Sphinx lurked near the long 4th and was wont to leap out at passing golfers with a riddle: "What claims to be 24, is apparently 16, but ends as 14?"

She cursed all who failed to answer correctly with a vicious slice for life, and it was not until R. Oedipus Broiles, the Houston Hacker, played here and answered the riddle that this dreaded scourge of the fairways was finally laid to rest. His answer? A cheater! He claims to play off a 24, shoots to a 16 to win his bets, but is cheopped to 14 when the club handicapper hears about him.

Gizeh — Egypt

THE DRAKENSBERG GOLF CLUB'S 9th

480 yards
par 3

DEVIL'S THIRST

IF DAMOCLES HAD BEEN A GOLFER instead of a swordsman, his Niblick would have been hanging over the Drakensberg Clubhouse last year — and all because of a flat tire.

During the '83 Phuthaditjhabe & Champagne Castle Hotel Pro-Am, the Jeep scheduled to transport essential liquid refreshments up to the Halfway House (just by the 10th tee) blew a tire while loading up at the Hotel.

Strangely, until that day not one complaint had been received about the steepish climb to the 9th: but when it was discovered that, on arrival, there was nothing available to drink . . .

The fate of the Club hung in the balance until Secretary Jules Oppenheimer pulled a family string or two and brought a helicopter in from Kimberley for an emergency airlift.

Devil's Tooth, Drakensberg's — South Africa

THE DIAMOND HEAD GOLF CLUB'S

3rd

490 yards
par 5

LITTLE RIPPER

NO ONE IN AUSTRALIA, with the possible exception of Bob Hawke, leans more to the left than did 4' 8" Jacques de Rippero. Apart from becoming Melbourne's youngest Communist (at age three and a half) and being born with his right leg 4" longer than its mate, Jacques espoused every leftist cause he could find. And when he was put up for membership at Diamond Head (his left side being put up 4" higher of course . . .) and being about as bright as a 3 watt bulb; he immediately bought a second-hand set of left-handed clubs. Even so, he managed to hole out the admittedly easy 1st in only 34, but when he attempted the somewhat more hazardous 3rd (see our photograph) his combination of handicaps proved too much. On the green in 42, Jacques was dismayed to see a bold approach putt from the top of the green run past and lodge in the middle of the swing bridge. As he lurched determinedly, if lopsidedly, after the ball, his putter tangled in his legs, causing him to topple into the foaming brine.

He did not, alas, resurface. The match committee, ever ready to honor dedication, named this hole in his memory.

Diamond Head — New South Wales, Australia

THE YOHO COUNTRY CLUB'S
1st

---

370 yards
par 4

THE HOODOOS

THE ONLY HAITIAN PROFESSIONAL (at least as far as the Canadian Circuit goes) to begin a National Open muttering strange incantations accompanied by a caddy playing a calypso version of Mozart's *Jupiter Symphony* on a 5-gallon gas can, was that 280-pound charmer "Mama Quack" Duvalier.

Asked by her bemused — and decidedly rattled — partner (a) why and (b) to desist immediately, Mama Q. explained that she'd been told this particular Open venue had been described to her as a voodoo course, and she was but taking natural precautions! When it was made clear that the local name around British Columbia for this type of golf course was "Hoodoos" and quite free from evil spirits, she quieted down and played in silence.

Quite free? *You* must play there and judge for yourself, for Mama Quack failed to make the cut!

Leauchoil Hoodoos — Yoho National Park, Canada

THE AGRA TOWN & COUNTRY CLUB'S PRACTICE PUTTING GREEN

85 yards x 6 yards

AGRA-VATION

THE CONVERSION, late in '83, of this fine old mausoleum into Agra's newest and most splendid clubhouse has also given members perhaps the finest practice putting green in the world.

Alas, though, no sooner was the inaugural competition (the Mumtaz Mahal Memorial Medal) under way than an unseemly incident took place here. Two visiting foursomes, from Australia and New Zealand respectively, faced a long wait before teeing off at the 10th and decided on a game of nine ball — best score round the putting green using a driver shaft as a billiard cue! A few beers were sunk and soon merriment turned into recrimination. Fortunately club pro Hamish McGhandi was a black belt in impassive resistance and it was the work of a moment for him to switch on the sprinklers and wade in among them, his putter flailing.

Tempers soon cooled but to this day no drinks are served until 18 holes have been completed.

Taj Mahal — India

THE KITA-HOTAKADAKE GOLF & CLIMBING CLUB'S

2nd

1082 yards
par 7

PEAKED

SUCH IS THE AVERAGE Japanese businessman's shortage of leisure time that when he finds a sporting club which allows him to combine two pleasures for the price of one, he is overjoyed.

Up here in the Alps, this lovely Nagano Club offers its lucky (if restricted) membership a combination of climbing and golfing such as is seldom seen in the Land of the Rising Sun. Agreed, after a comparatively easy 444 yard par 3 first, it is a little tough to find oneself faced with the longish carry required to make sense of this, the real introductory hole of the course. Fortunately, many of the players who have the stamina actually to reach the tee are content to thump a desultory drive or two into the chasm then retire, physically and morally satisfied (not to mention exhausted) to the clubhouse for a well-earned flask or two of saki.

Mt. Kita-Hotakodake — Nagnao Pre. Japan

THE YESNABY CASTLE MUNICIPAL LINKS
6th

---

210 yards
par 3

MODRED'S LOT

IN THE TRUE DARK AGES, during those years which followed the infamous Royal edict against "The Playing of the Gowf", when the King's men ranged far and wide apprehending anyone who spoke too loosely in taverns of how he played the long 15th last weekend, there crept into our language those dread words "Bogey-men", or "The beating of the Bogey". But even then, far to the north, a tiny band of low-handicap dissidents stood firm against the Crown, the treacherous waters of the Pentland Firth forming a buffer of safety.

The nights in the Orkney Islands being as long as they are, a nucleus of Twilight Golfers grew around the fine natural links at Yesnaby. Leader of this brave band was none other than the legendary Modred Bews who, when in form, would take his usual hook here at the 6th, then using his famous cable-throwing prowess, hurl clubs, bag and golf cart across the gap onto the green, dive down into the seething cauldron below, swim over, climb up and, to the rapturous cheers of his regular gallery, putt out — often for a birdie. This hole is in fact named in posthumous honor of Modred's final, unsuccessful dive, taken at low tide during the last round of the Stronsay Open of '45.

Orkney Islands — Scotland

THE CANYONS COUNTRY CLUB'S 1st

405 yards
par 4

SWINGERS

THIS DELIGHTFUL GOLF HOLE, the first at Canyons, is surely the finest way to begin a round. Not too long, an easy par if the ball is struck accurately, an exhilarating view over the course and an ideal preparation for the testing long second (par 6), the tee of which is seen lower right. Though a certain lissomeness of limb is advantageous here, it is thanks to the foresight of prominent course architect Snr. García L. de Cárdenas who in a preliminary survey of the site for future course layout back in 1540, left copious notes on locations for swing bridges and rope ladders, thus today enabling more elderly players to enjoy a quiet round. The recommended approach here is a full wood to the central plateau, then a lofted mid-iron *with plenty of spin on the ball* up to the pin. Take care not to overclub as a too-low shot could roll right over the normally hard-surfaced green, and a valuable stroke or two be lost playing back up.

Grand Canyon — Arizona, America

THE LAKE QUILL COUNTRY CLUB'S 10th

---

635 yards
par 2

QUILL'S FOLLY

PURISTS HAVE ARGUED THAT 635 yards could be considered a trifle long for a par 2; yet there have been more holes-in-one here than on any other hole in our series! During a well-earned holiday break from his memorable nationwide tour in '87, concert pianist Eugene Quills (no relation) cleverly used his putter off the tee, rolling his ball into the waterfall to gain carry to the green. Alas, by the time he descended to green level his ball had been carried over five miles downstream and he finally putted out for a card-spoiling 986.

Sutherland Falls — New Zealand

Golf Holes 55 — 72

THE STONEHENGE COUNTRY CLUB'S 18th

412 yards
par 4

SACRI LEDGE

MANY THE PRINTED dissertation on this, the most venerable of England's country clubs; how little though we have found out of its origins, shrouded as they are in the misty past of golf's very beginnings. Yet: if it hadn't been for that curious coincidence at the '57 Architect's Invitation Best Ball, we'd be even more in the dark. The identification by A.J.M. McAretz (Royal P.G.A.) of the now world-famous chalky white drawing on the stone which supports the 18th green as an early Neolithic baffie brought two elderly historians to blows. And when he followed this up next round with a badly topped drive which chipped away a fragment of stone at the base to reveal part of a runic inscription, there was even a letter to The Times (unpublished owing to a union dispute).

Roughly translated, the runes tell of an event known then as "The Archdruid's Chalice", and three times mentions the names Stan and Boadicea Hengist. That the standing stones were originally laid out as a tight little golf course, and that the event in question was obviously a mixed pairs tournament, is no longer a point of contention. But the suggestion that the course was named in honor of 3-times winner Stan Hengist is still arguable.

Stonehenge — England

THE KAROO COUNTRY CLUB'S 14th

840 yards
par 6

KOPPIE CAT

THOUGH THERE IS A GREEN FEE facility at this old established Club, the attention of visitors should be drawn to the somewhat ominous guide book comment that *"There are as yet no facilities for tourists"*. However, golfers with the courage of their sporting convictions will not hesitate to brave the rigors of what is surely one of the loveliest courses in the world — made lovelier (if more difficult!) by the abundance of wildlife which graces its 200+ acres; Zebra, Gemsbok, Haretebeest, Wildebeest and Springbok may often be spotted from the flat-topped hills which comprise many of the tees and greens.

As indeed may the odd lion, as old Ebeneezer van der Merwe found to his disadvantage late one evening here at the long 14th. That he still lives to tell the tale is due only to his excellent short iron game — a point seldom stressed in your average instruction manual!

Karoo — South Africa

THE MOUNT PILATUS GOLF CLUB'S 9th

540 yards
par 5

PILATE ERROR

AS A RULE, golfing anecdotes in Swiss 19ths don't always make the blood race. Something in the national character seems to turn out golfers who seldom stray far from handicaps in the 8-15 area. But as though to prove the rule, visitors to this fine mountain club are invariably thrilled to hear the tale of old William "Four-Eyes" Tell, at his very best never below a 36 handicap. Though powerful, he had problems with alignment, and couldn't putt for beans. But even Will had hidden reserves . . . one day out on the practice fairway, he was duffing 9-irons quite happily, his son picking up balls for him, when out of the blue the youngster screamed in terror! Looking up quickly (and thereby hitting his first clean ball of the day) Will saw what seemed to be a ghostly figure above his son's head, dressed in a toga and continually washing his hands.

Rightly guessing this to be the spirit of Pontius Pilate (whose body had been thrown into a nearby lake some years before) William whipped out his 1-wood, teed up three balls and blasted them clean through the wraith, not even scratching the boy! "One for the father, one for the son — and take that, you bloody ghost!" snarled William as he struck superb drives. After the 3rd ball the apparition disappeared. A close shave indeed!

Mt. Pilatus — Switzerland

THE KRAKATOA GOLF CLUB'S
16th

410 yards
par 4

CRACK UP

THE CURIOUS CONFIGURATIONS of Krakatoa command careful consideration by even the most competent of golfers — despite its current comparatively somnambulistic state it can create problems not normally encountered on your average course.

No doubt, it caused something of an eruption in local golfing circles when the new layout was unveiled back in 1883, and it retains still that unique facility of rearranging itself from time to time. Visitors can never be sure if the long 8th still has that fiendish dogleg — or indeed if it is still there at all.

It all makes for an exciting style of golf peculiar to this part of the world.

Krakatoa — Indonesia

THE OTTER CREST COUNTRY CLUB'S 18th

620 yards
par 5

ROTTER

THE MAIN DIFFERENCE between this demanding 18th and its counterpart at Pebble Beach is that here there is no "easy road" for the higher handicapper to take, content with a bogey to end his round. It's all or nothing (though a recovery *can* be made at low tide, depending on how deeply the ball plugs in).

A quick warning here to those who like to play at lunch or end of day — beware the giant otters who lurk in caves by the rocks. Their voracious appetites have curtailed many a decent round.

Otter Crest — Oregon, America

THE AORANGI COUNTRY CLUB'S
6th

390 yards
par 4

CHASM

A TEST EVEN FOR BIG HITTERS (who too often sacrifice accuracy for distance) but easier than it looks because of the elevated tee; Club Captain Angus McAngus, whose noted monograph (soon to be translated into Hindi, Swahili and Gaelic) proves that golf balls fly further per cubic inch of applied muscle at heights above 3041 yards, regularly drives this green, cunningly using the tussock grass above the pin as a backstop.

His brother Igor, Vice Captain and amateur aviator (seen in the picture) owns the world's largest collection of frozen golf balls.

Mt. Cook National Park — New Zealand

THE YINCHÜAN GOLF CLUB'S 8th

440 yards
par 4

WALL OF DEATH

WHEN CHINA SO RECENTLY decided to burst into the 20th century with a series of major international deals, only a surprisingly small proportion of the Western media made mention of the magnificent redesigning of the ancient Yinchüan course. Laid out along the 1490 miles of the Great Wall, it offered, with fairways seldom more than 12 feet wide, a potent test of straight hitting and careful green work.

Originally designed to protect Chinese members from ravening hordes of non-green-fee-paying Northern Barbarians, the layout was and is famous for its series of turreted half-way houses. The course record (8247) is still held by General Kash Mai Chek, whose habit of beheading anyone who disagreed with his tally ensured excellent cards.

Great Wall — China

THE TANAH LOT COUNTRY CLUB'S
17th

408 yards
par 4

SOFTLY SOFTLY

LOCAL RULES AND CUSTOMS are an integral part of golf's infinite allure; that they must be respected and adhered to at all times is understood — no one wants to drop an unnecessary shot — but from time to time they may also be enjoyed as an art form in themselves.

A major and fascinating feature of this distinguished seaside links is shown in our photograph. The "Kechak" or Caddy Dance, held on the 17th fairway, precedes every major tournament.

Though its origins are shrouded in the mists of the club's beginnings, today its primary function is to allocate caddies to players. The competitor must walk out on the fairway with his clubs, for inspection, and at a signal from the clubhouse the first hand in the air is successful. To the casual visitor it can be unnerving — but assuredly interesting.

Bali — Indonesia

THE SHENANDOAH COUNTRY CLUB'S 12th

405 yards
par 4

GETTY WHO?

SKYLINE DRIVE (seen in the distance) runs along more than 100 miles of Virginia's famous Blue Ridge Mountains; yet no sight equals in splendor the entrancing little golf course nestling high above the river.

Little, but not easy! Professionals give it a wide berth (lest they spoil their averages) and the course record of 98, has been held (since 1862) by the legendary T.J. "Longball" Jackson when he trounced elderly Henry "Light-Horse Harry" Lee during the Senior Champs.

Harry's son, young Bobby, never forgave Jackson for this humiliating defeat, and indeed his antagonism in the years to come almost mounted to a campaign against that fine golfer!

Shenandoah National Park — Western Virginia, America

THE RUAPEHU GOLF CLUB INC.'S
2nd

685 yards
par 5

CRATER LUCK

NEW ZEALAND'S SNOWY UPLANDS have long held a fascination for those golfers keen to experiment with unusual hazards, and here in R.G.C.'s first nine is one of golf's strangest tests. Assistant Greenkeeper Ethelred McMurtrie's singular discovery that grass could be grown on ice due to a weird combination of Crater Lake minerals and a certain temperature has meant that, quite suddenly and unpredictably, the famous lake turns into a green. Golfers from far and near line up for the privilege of playing this unique challenge, but as the green seldom stays playable for longer than an hour or two, many are disappointed. Indeed some are quite distressed, for despite a local rule stating that no more than two players may putt out at the same time, the tendency for boiling water beneath to melt unexpected segments of green has meant the sudden disappearance of more than one golfer intent on lining up a birdie, often with scarce a cry.

Mt. Ruapehu — New Zealand

THE DUTCH CREEK GOLF CLUB'S

11th

320 yards
par 4

? COURAGE

THOUGH IMMIGRANTS from the Netherlands have made their marks (or if you prefer, their guilders) in many parts of the North American continent, very few travelled as far as British Columbia before putting down roots.

Luckily for today's keen golfers, one who did was retired inebriate Jan van der Baffie, whose family connections made it appropriate that he open the first mountain links in the province.

Unfortunately his love affair with anything in a bottle over 2% alcohol led him to design some spectacularly difficult holes. But, all in all, the now immensely popular course here is an outstanding tribute to a thoroughly ordinary man.

Dutch Creek — British Columbia, Canada

THE SHUKKEIEN COUNTRY CLUB'S
12th

---

105 yards
par 3

STOP-GO

THE PLACID SERENITY of these idyllic Japanese gardens offers a true golfing paradise. At just under 4000 yards it isn't the longest course in the world, but it can lay claim to being not only the prettiest, but the most liberally supplied with refreshment stops.

Known locally as "No. 19's", these essential adjuncts to any civilized golf course are placed at every second green. This is in part due to the larger than usual number of par 3's (11) which create hold-ups on busy days, in part to the natural desire of every red-blooded golfer to utilize all moments not actually involving striking a ball in battling dehydration caused by over exertion.

Shukkeien Gardens — Hiroshima, Japan

THE MT. KINABALU COUNTRY CLUB'S 18th

380 yards
par 4

TOP HOLE

TUCKED AWAY UP NORTH in the Sabah Province of Borneo, seldom appreciated by tourists but beloved of its members, lies one of the few golf courses in the world laid out over the slopes of a volcano.

At about a good 1-iron over 4000 yards, the atmospheric 18th (one of the highest last holes in existence) tends to make first-time visitors draw a sharp breath. (If, that is, they can draw any breath at all, at that height!) The major difficulty here is learning to cope with bounces off the lava fairways. Though in contrast, the greens, thanks to a $\frac{1}{4}$ inch of grass over smooth stone, are like billiard tables. In fact, some of them have been removed to *become* billiard tables!

This fine old Club has long fought for the privilege of holding the Southeast Asia Open, but one reason alone has prevented this:

Men's clubhouse lore notwithstanding, there is no such thing as an extinct volcano!

Mt. Kinabalu — Borneo

THE RUSSELL FALLS COUNTRY CLUB'S 9th

390 yards
par 4

THE SHROUDS

WHEN PEOPLE'S GOLF HERO Dmitri "Big Brucie" Bryusov, morally neutered after nearly making second last in the Albanian Open, recovered his senses to find himself part of a mixed foursome here at Russell Falls, he was at a loss for words. How were his friends to know when they tossed him into the back seat of a cab that they'd chosen the only Australian driver in Tirana? And as the cabbie, "Aussie" Obradovic, could only speak a Sydney dialect of Serbo-Croat he'd quite understandably mistaken the slurred command "Taman Peninsula" for "Tasman". Spotting the matched set of Autographed Niklauskis and hoping for a fat tip he'd driven straight there. But it was not to be Big Brucie's day. Wordlessly driving off into the picturesque "Shrouds" he was astonished to see an extremely voracious marsupial snatch the ball in powerful jaws and disappear into the bush. As this was a K.G.B. Special (with built-in recording device) Brucie was never again totally at ease in the Kremlin — or indeed in Hobart!

CROC TRAP

Russell Falls — Tasmania, Australia

THE BLYDE RIVER CANYON GOLF CLUB'S 2nd

650 yards
par 5

THREE DEVILS

THE FAMOUS THREE ROUND DEVILS — or "Rondavels" as they are known in Afrikaans — offer an awesome challenge to even the most powerful of hitters.

The 2nd here is believed to be the only South African golf hole with a fixed tee and three alternative greens, the flag position being determined at the whim of Assistant Greenkeeper Bosambo McBotha, whose ability to scamper agilely up and down the sheer greensides like a veritable monkey is not altogether a coincidence.

It is not generally touted about, but assuredly worth remembering, that for a mere Krugerrand Bosambo will alter pin position to suit any given drive — an interesting variation on the American "Mulligan"!

Three Rondavels — South Africa

THE SIR ADAM BECK GENERATING STATION'S PRIVATE GOLF CLUB'S
11th

380 yards
par 4

DRY DOCK

THIS PRIVATE COURSE has to be one of the least played in America, spending as it does so much of its time underwater. In the early days, before it became a tourist attraction and a major hydroelectric plant, and it was discovered that visiting tourists — most of whom seemed to be on honeymoon — preferred watching the waterfall to playing a round (though in some parts of the world quite the opposite is the case) it was a popular sporting arena for Canadians and Americans alike.

Today it is rare that the water level is low enough to permit competitive play — and even then most members prefer looking for previously lost balls. Something else, incidentally, which also attracts the honeymooners . . .

Niagara Falls — America

THE GRAMPIAN GOLF CLUB'S

5th

85 yards
par 3

VERTIGOOOₒₒₒ

BELIEVED TO BE the world's only vertical par 3, this shortish hole demands not only pin-point accuracy but exceptional balance too; most players favor a wedge off the tee, scooping the ball high into the air to land squarely on the awkwardly contoured green. Should the ball fail to stay up it may (with luck) fall back to its point of origin (sometimes stunning the slower-moving golfer) or it may fall even farther as, alas, did "Mad Dan" Mackintosh, the Melbourne Maestro, who in a practice round in '21 played just a fraction too much off his back foot, lost his equilibrium and followed his ball into the abyss. Years later a passing Boy Scout troop found a decaying mashie-niblick in the valley below, but of "Mad Dan" nothing has been heard since. Though his voice may be heard if you tumble off the sloping green, "You'll come a-golfing Matilda with me."

Grampian Mts. — Victoria, Australia

THE SINGAPORE ISLAND COUNTRY CLUB'S

17th

480 yards
par 4

SNAP

THE SAD SAD CASE OF CROCODILE BILL still strikes terror into the hearts of young golfers lucky enough, while enjoying a beer at the splendid 19th, to fall into conversation with the garrulous Oldest Member. Way back during the formative years of the Club (when there was but one 18-hole layout), Bill would lurk in the Halfway House in wait for unsuspecting visitors who'd had a good first 9. How Bill plied them with a few Singapore Slings, got them into a heavy wager and invariably cleaned up was his own secret. And what happened that monsoon day in December 1940 will never be fully known.

We do know that Bill (it had to happen) had taken on a bigger crocodile than himself; and in desperation he'd doubled the stakes on the last hole; and that he still wasn't down after playing 6. To his final credit, rather than concede the match and pay up, Bill took the decent way out. Armed only with his putter he walked steadfastly forward to tap in.

This photograph was taken moments afterward by the Club Captain, fortunately looking out of the window at the time. On its evidence the Greens Committee had the hole redesigned a few yards further from the Crocodile Farm.

Crocodile Farm — Singapore

PRICE/STERN/SLOAN *Publishers, Inc.*
410 North La Cienega Boulevard, Los Angeles, California 90048